THE GREAT ARTISTS
Frida Kahlo

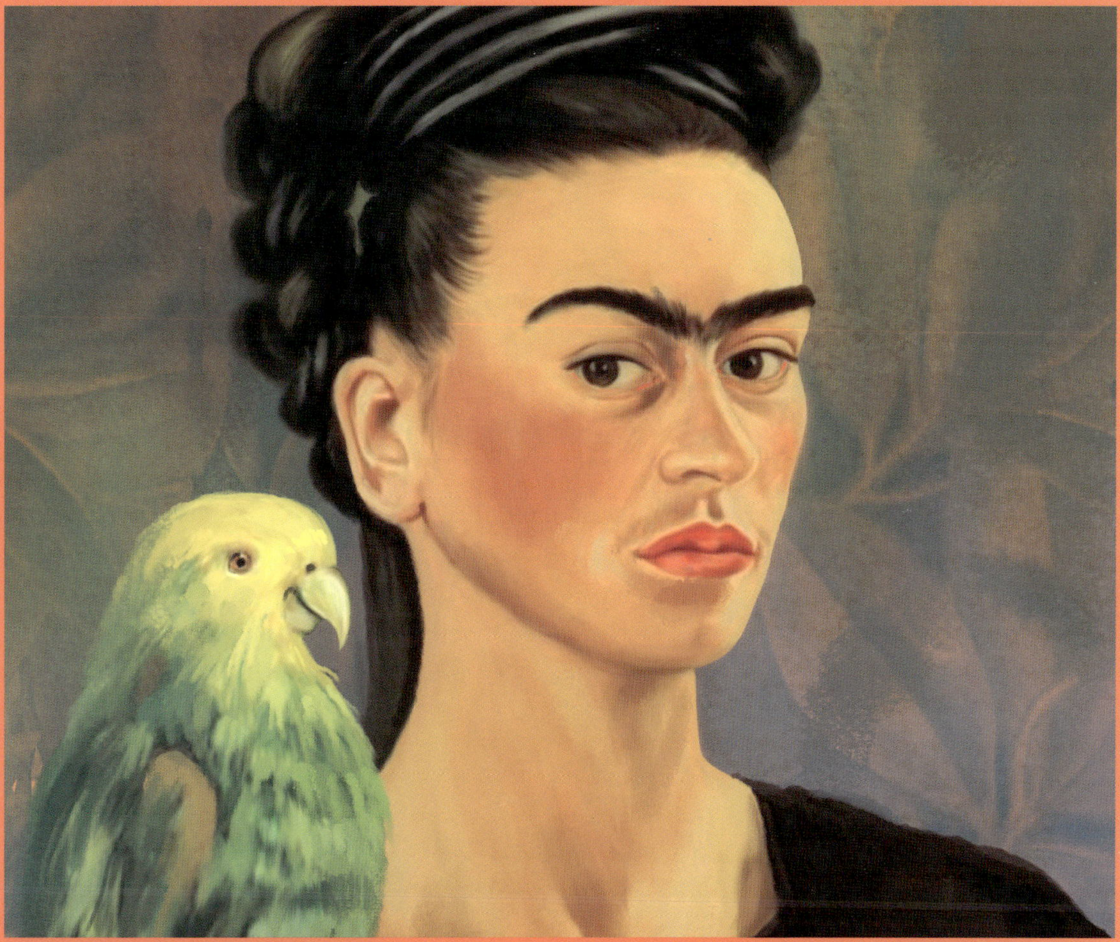

Anjali Raghbeer

Om KIDZ
An imprint of Om Books International

Frida sketched furiously in her notebook.

How can they be so mean? she thought. *They are ugly and stupid, not me.*

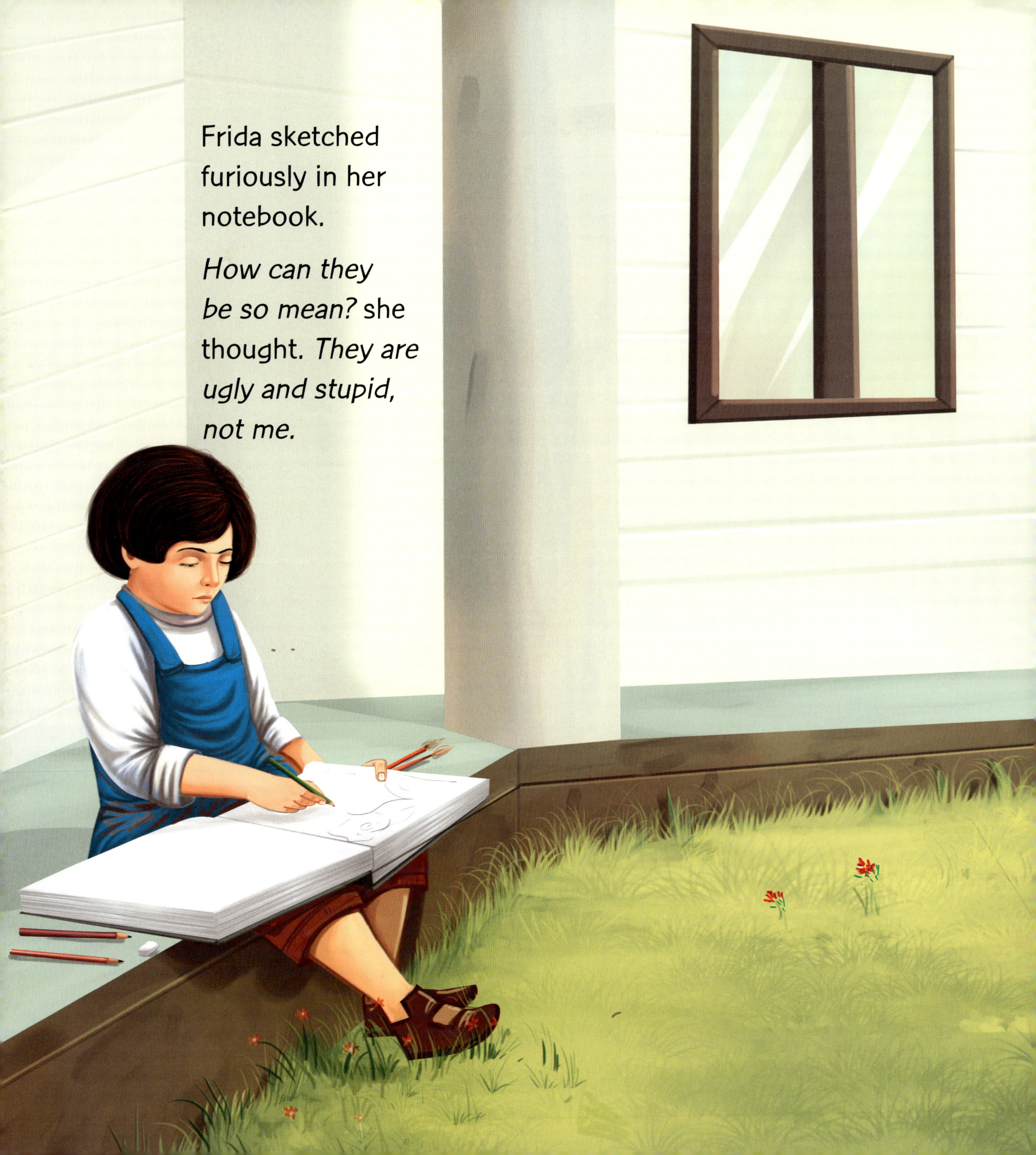

Polio had left her with one leg shorter than the other; she walked with a limp. Everyone in school made fun of her.

The only way she could drown out the sound of the taunts was with sketching.

I hate them, I will be better than any of them, one day, thought Frida.

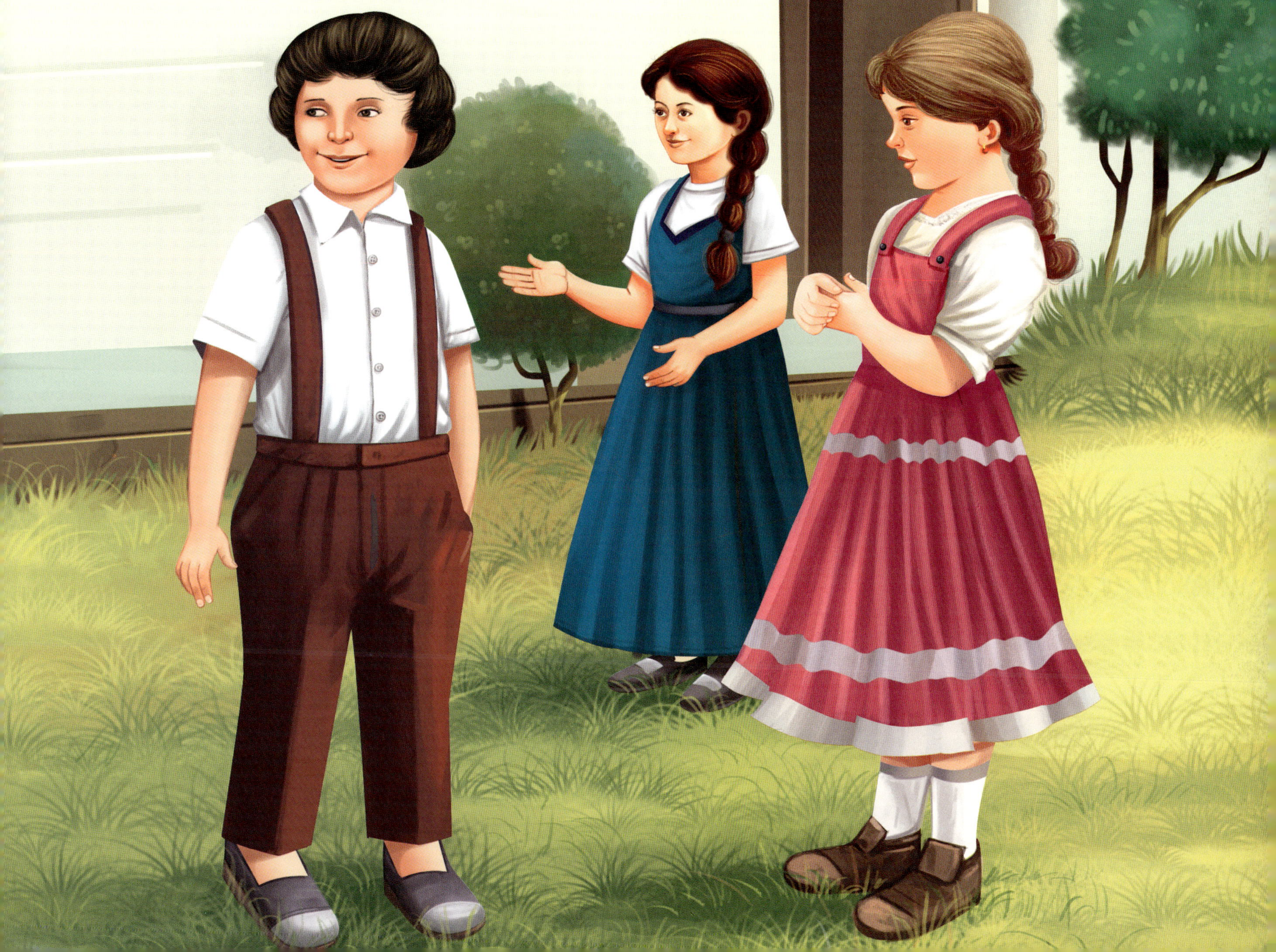

Frida entered the dark room in the corner of the house. She adjusted her eyes quickly to see her father bent over the glass plates he worked with to develop photographs.

'Wow,' she said, as she smelt the sharp silver salts he used.

It was the photograph of a beautiful cathedral in Mexico.

'Frida, do you want to learn how to make photographs today?' asked Guillermo, Frida's father.

'Yes, father!' squealed Frida.

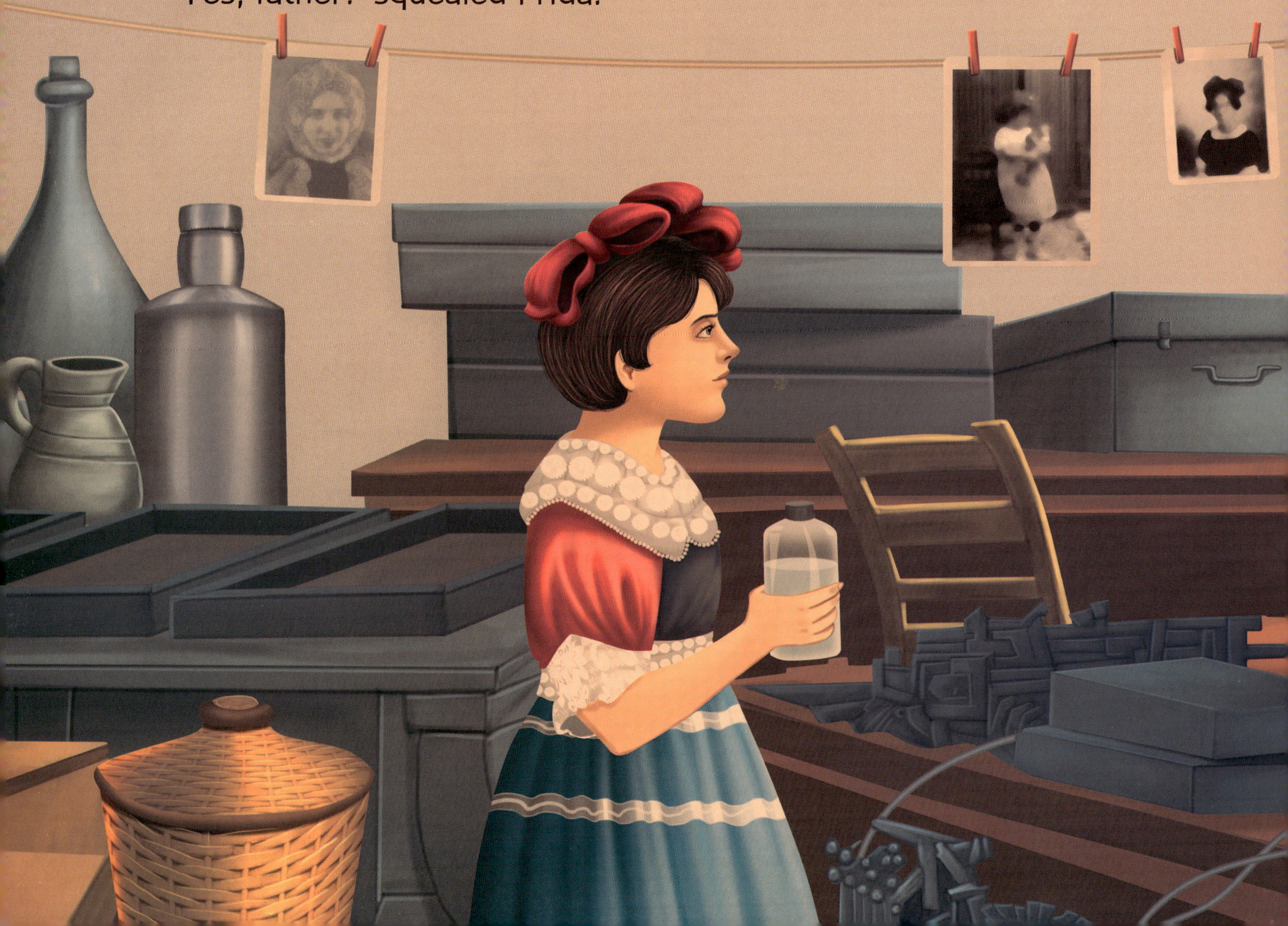

She observed carefully how her father used special colours to make photographs look good.

Every time Frida felt sad, she came and helped her father. Soon she became an expert in colouring photographs.

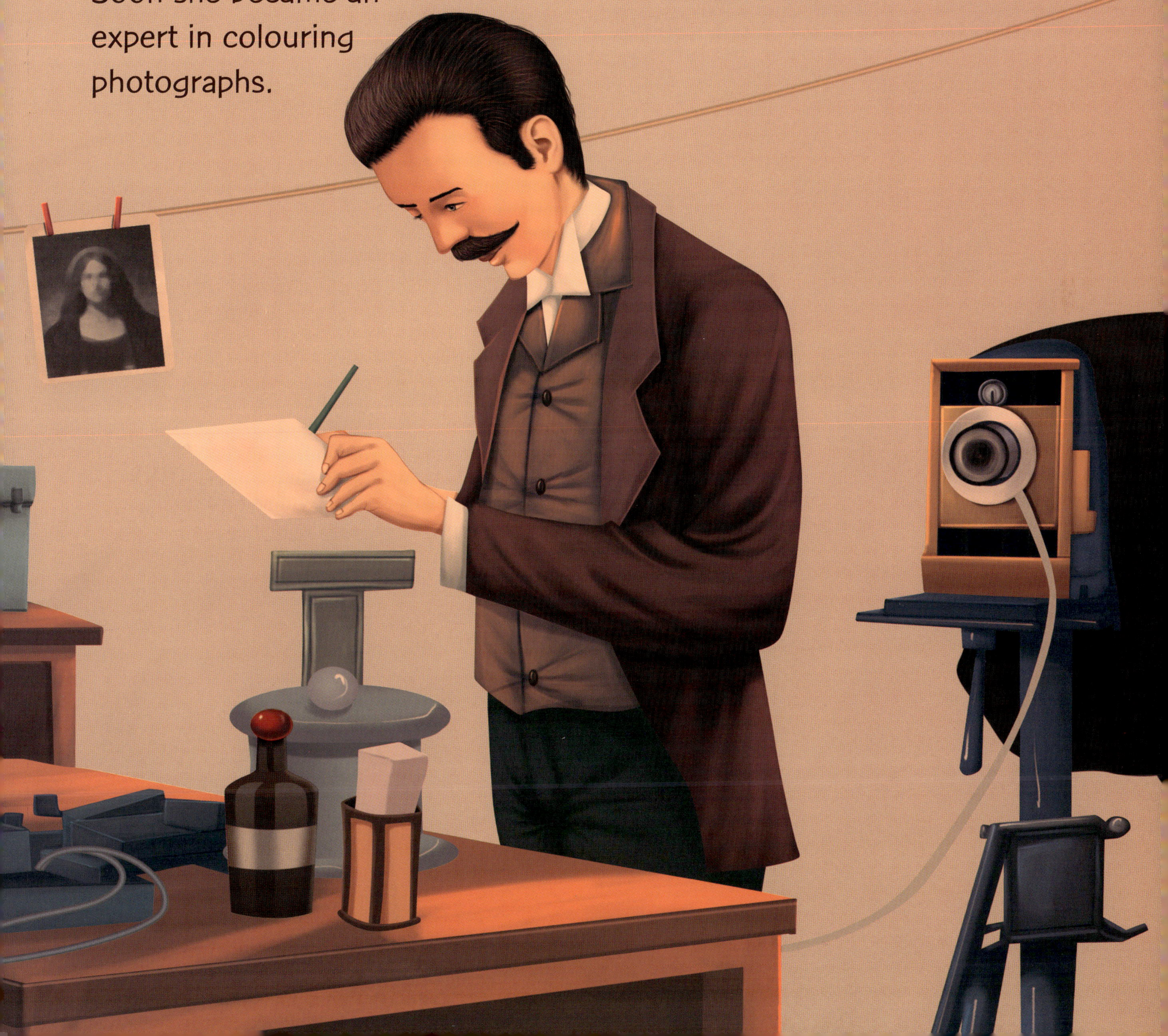

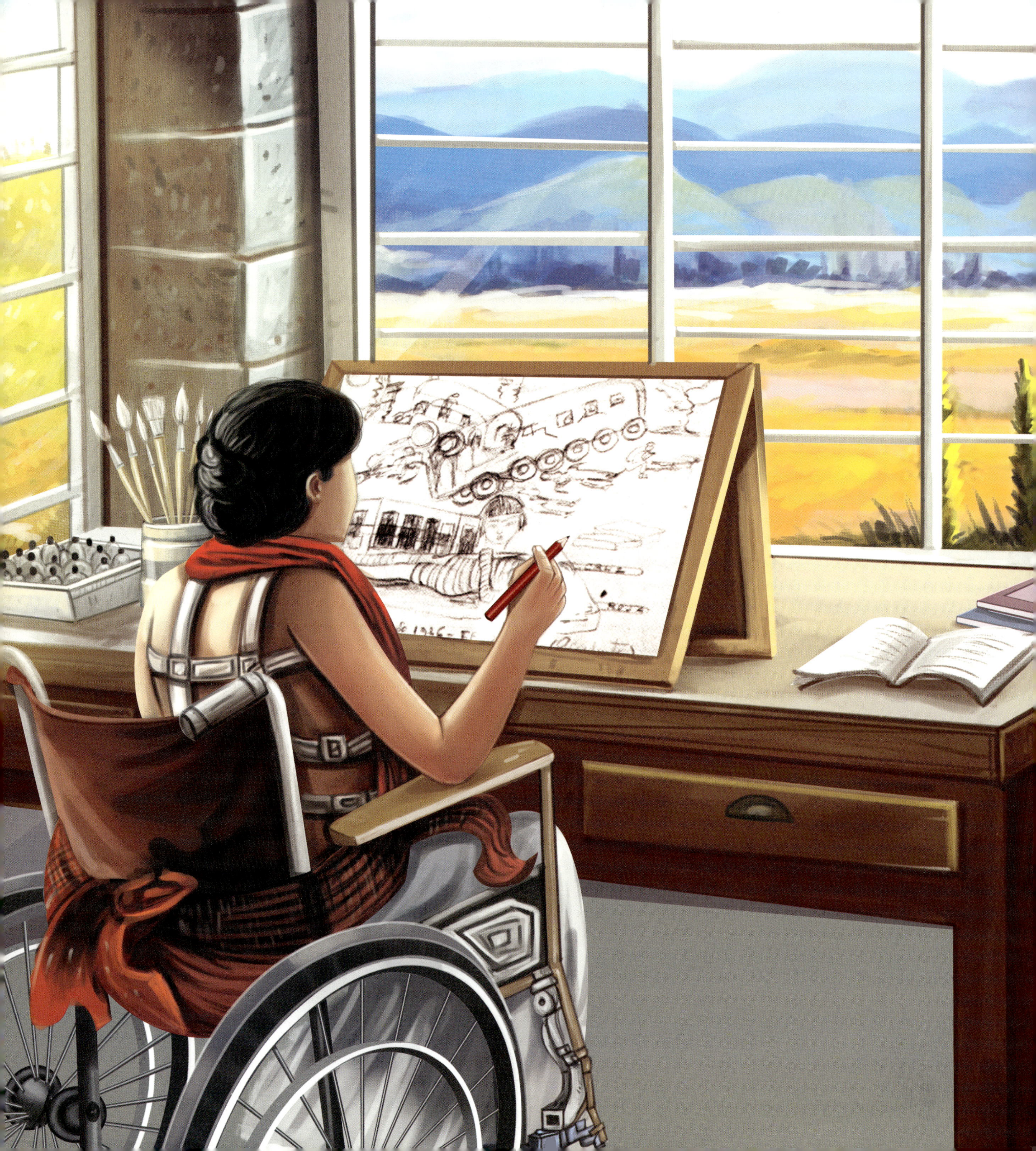

When Frida was older, she went to the National Preparatory School.

One day, Frida boarded the bus to go home with her best friend, Alex, after spending the day in Mexico City.

They sat together at the back of the bus.

Suddenly, everyone started to scream all at once.

'Trolley! Trolley!'

Frida looked up to see a street trolley hurtling toward her.

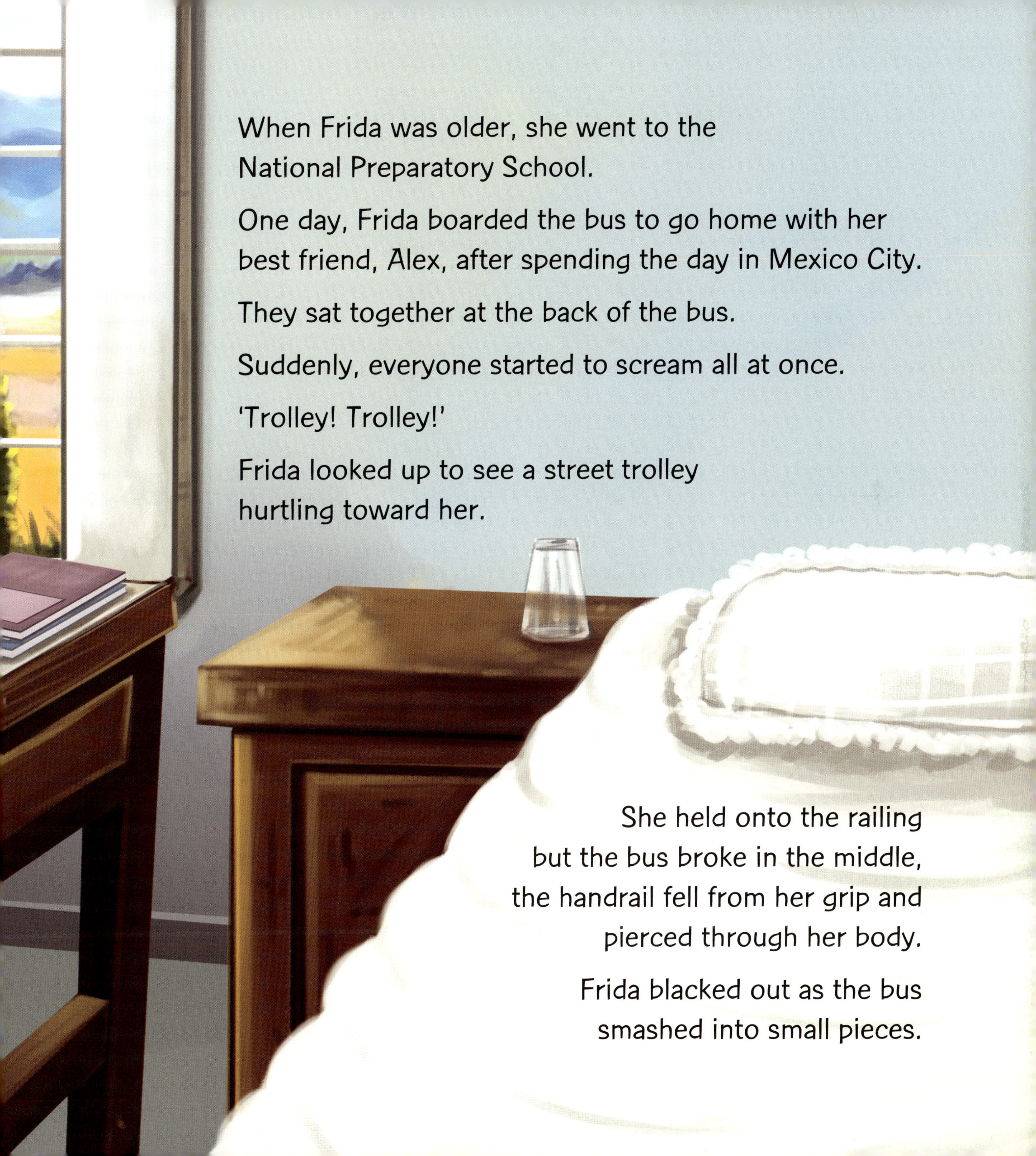

She held onto the railing but the bus broke in the middle, the handrail fell from her grip and pierced through her body.

Frida blacked out as the bus smashed into small pieces.

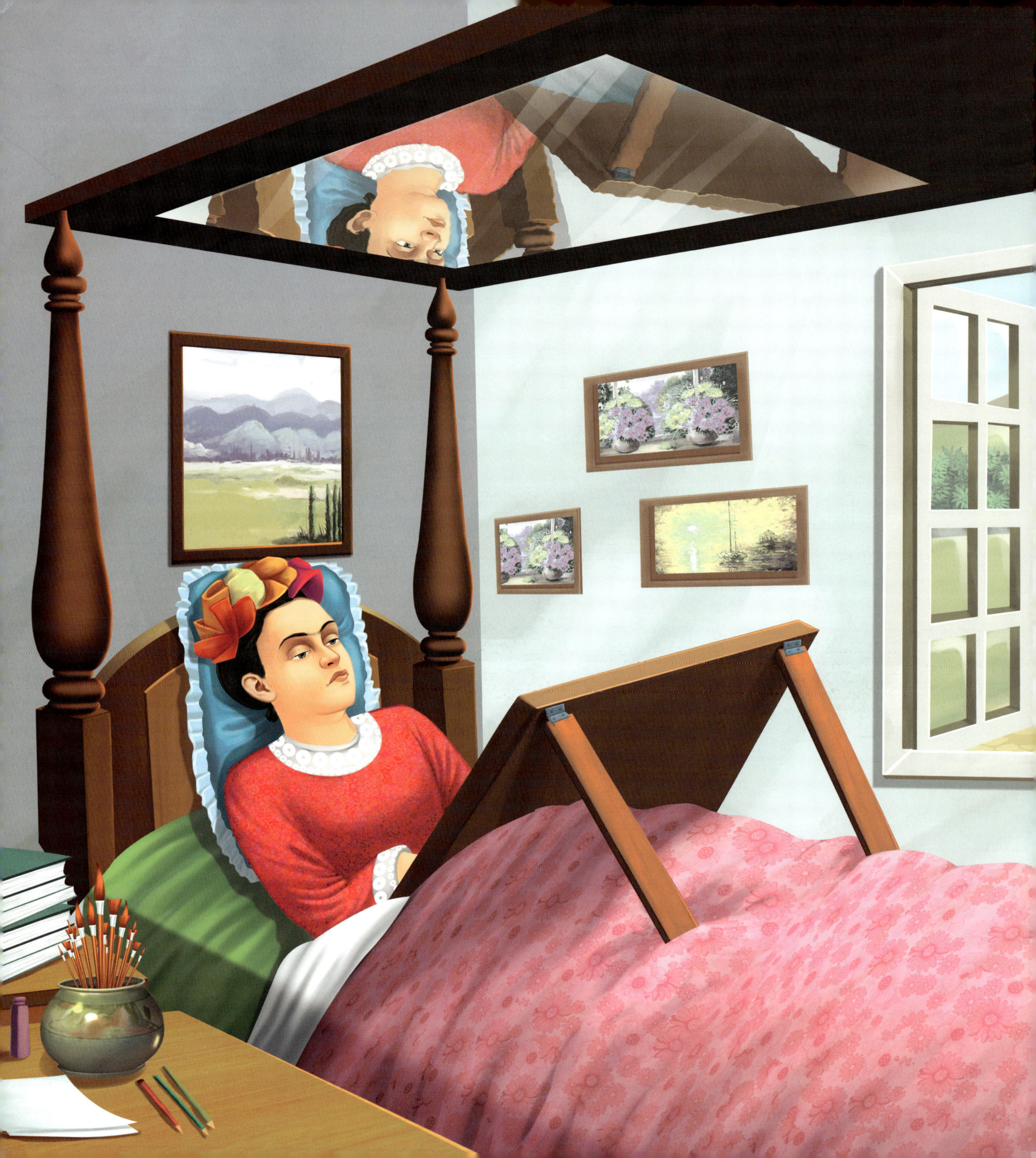

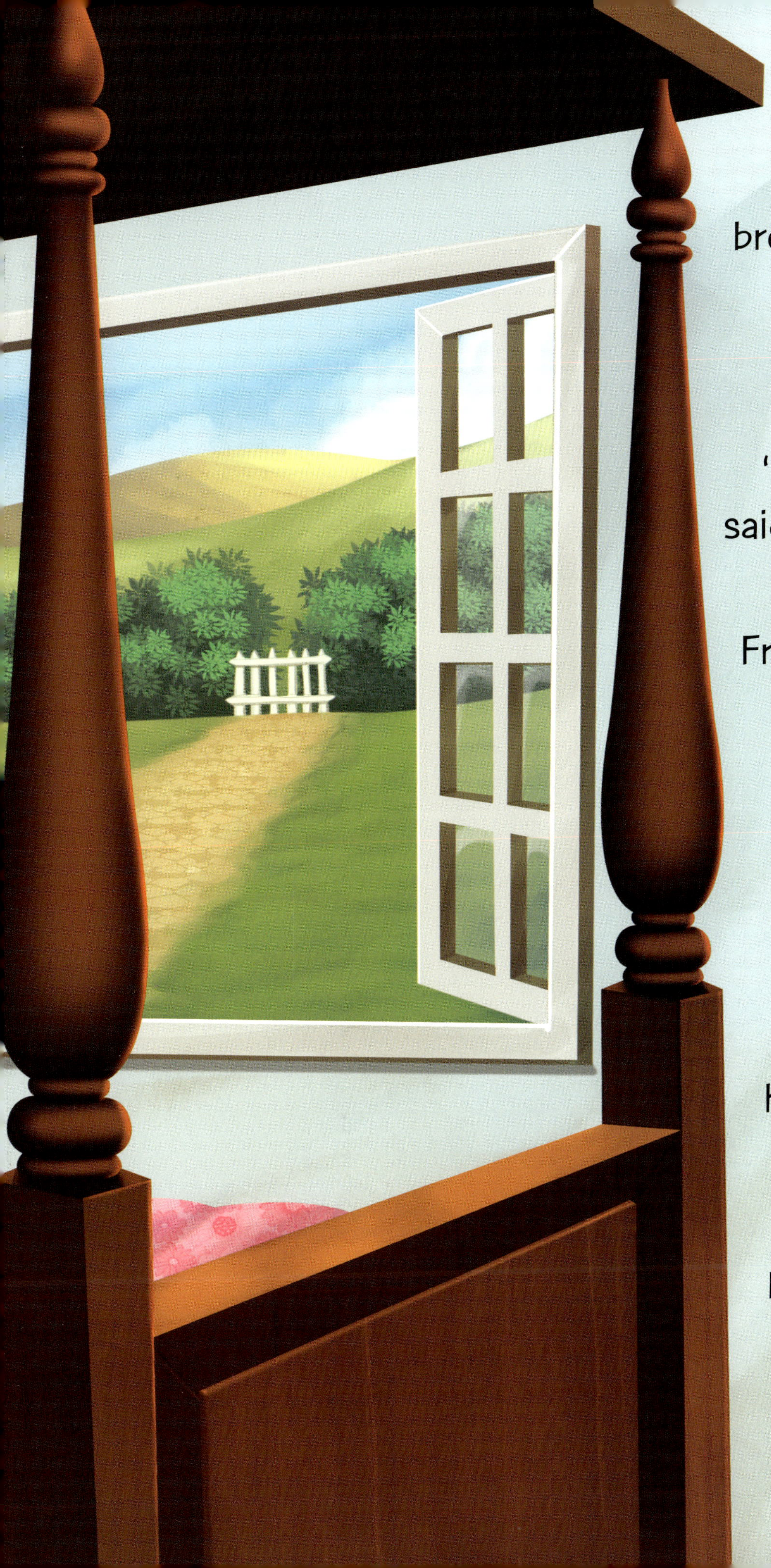

The accident left Frida with a broken spine and ribs. Her left leg was fractured in eleven places, while her right foot had got dislocated.

'Frida, I have a surprise for you,' said her mother through her tears.

She took out a small easel that Frida could use while lying down.

Frida threw the easel aside.

'I want to get out of bed,' she cried.

'Patience my dear, patience,' said her mother.

Frida had a mirror placed over her head so that she could paint her reflection.

It took two years for Frida to pull herself out of that state and even then she never became completely alright.

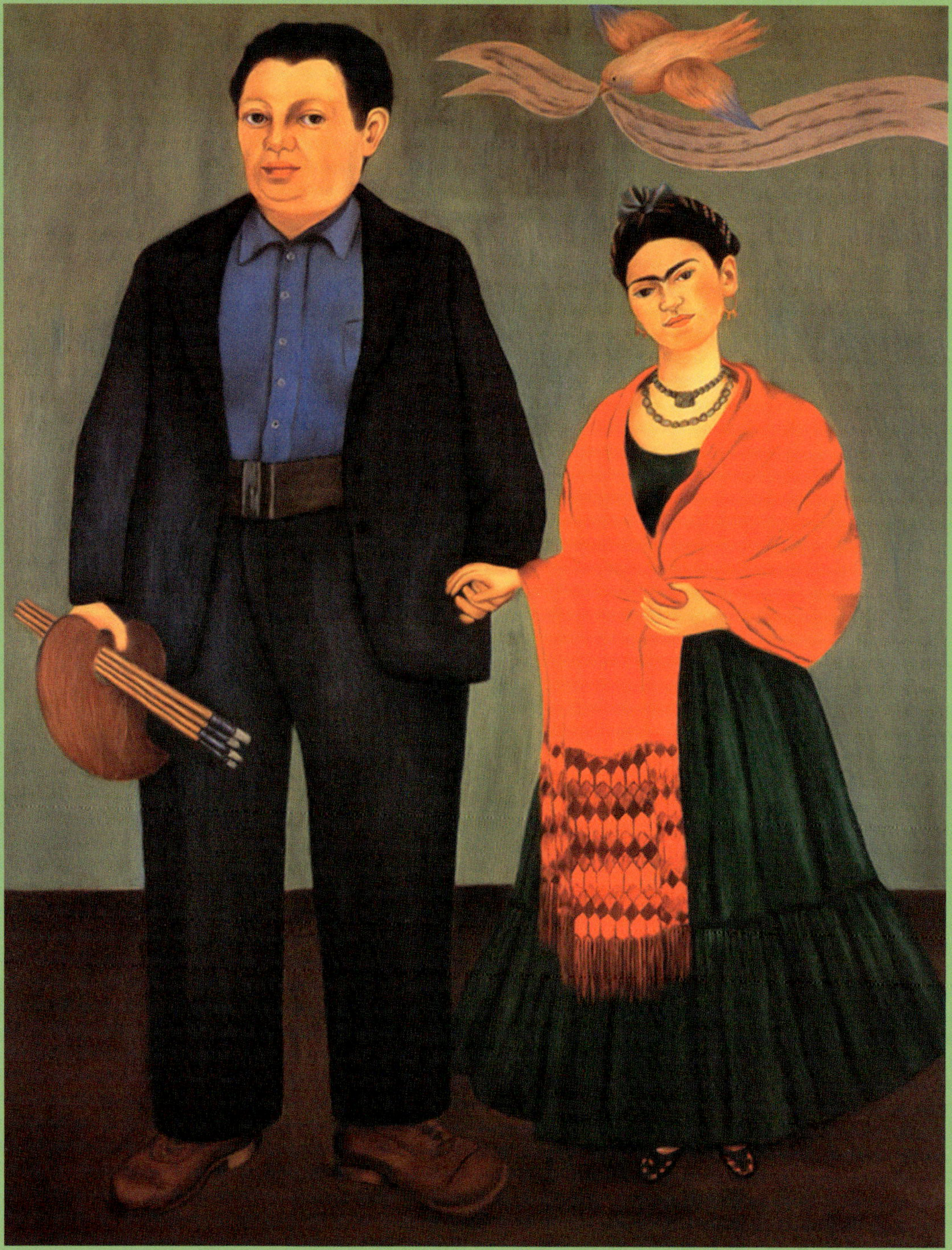

Soon after her recovery from the terrible accident, Frida went to Diego.

'Are my paintings any good?' she asked, spreading her work across his entire room.

'Yes, they are as beautiful as you,' said Diego.

Soon Diego and Frida were in love.

'I want to marry Diego,' announced Frida to her family.

'He is too old for you! You will be miserable,' shouted her father.

'I don't care,' said Frida. She wanted to meet new people. Diego showed her a world that was different from hers. With him, life would be an adventure.

He was the most famous artist she had ever before met.

After many arguments, Frida called Diego to the house to meet her father.

'She is sick. Why do you want to marry her?' said her father to Diego.

But Diego was adamant. He was madly in love with Frida.

Frida planned the wedding carefully and they were married on 21 August, 1929.

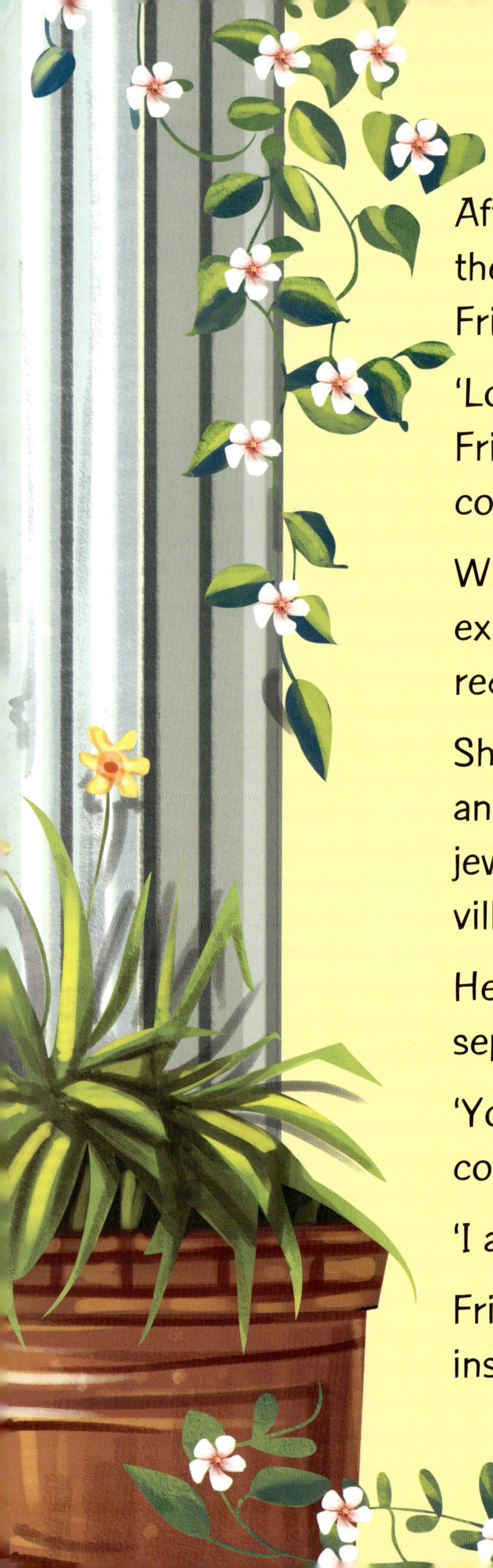

After marriage, Diego moved to a small village in the interiors of Mexico for a painting assignment. Frida went with him.

'Look at these paintings on the walls,' said Frida as she looked up and down at the brightly coloured paintings.

While Diego painted, Frida found herself exploring Mexican folk art. She loved the bold reds and blues and yellows.

She bought herself long skirts, did her hair up and wore colourful headgear. She wore heavy jewellery like the peasant women she saw in the villages of Mexico.

Her bushy eyebrows which did not have any separation made her look even more striking.

'You look lovely,' said Diego, boosting Frida's confidence to be herself even more.

'I am proud to be Mexican,' announced Frida.

Frida painted harder. She started putting symbols inside her work to give them different meanings.

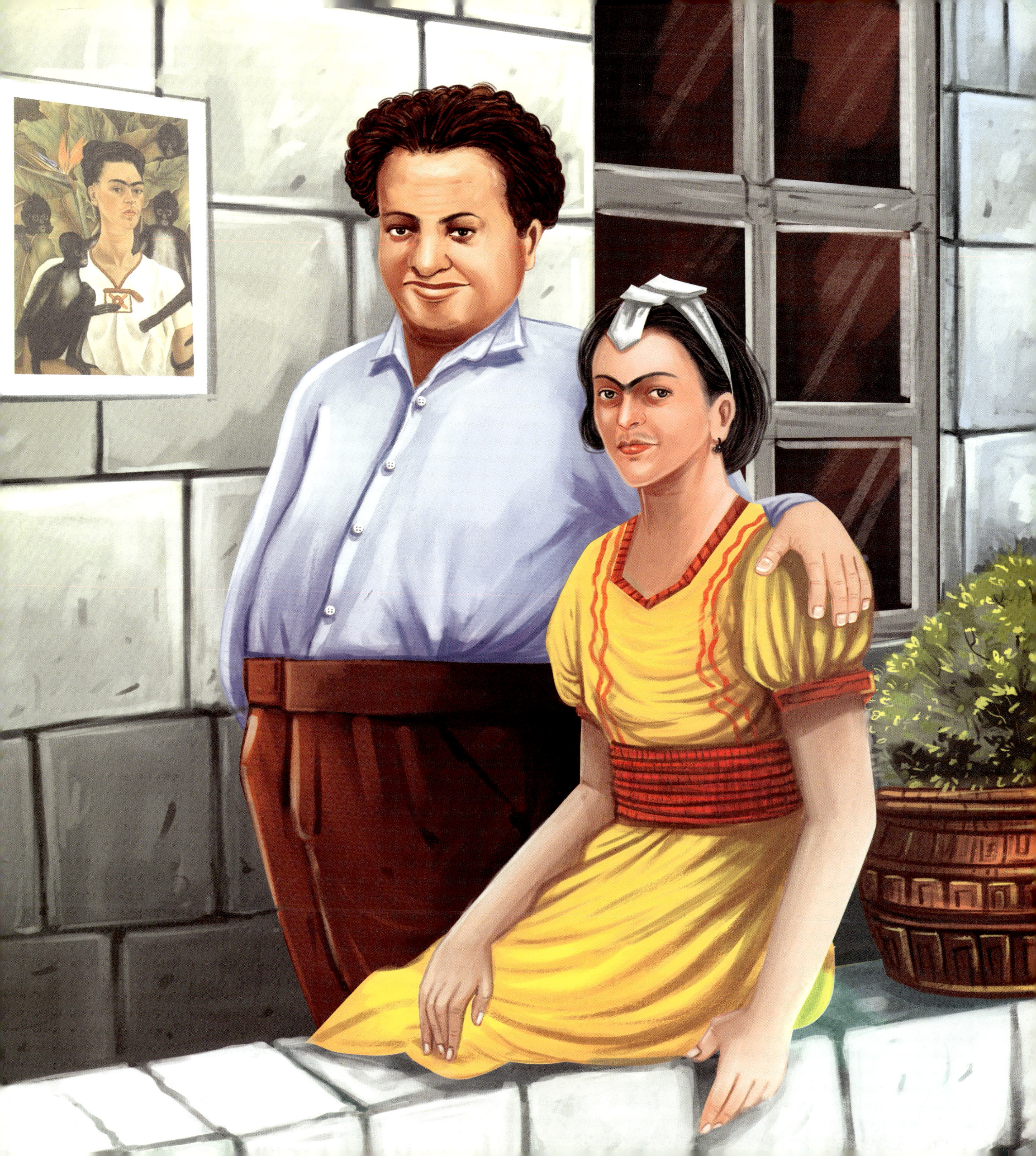

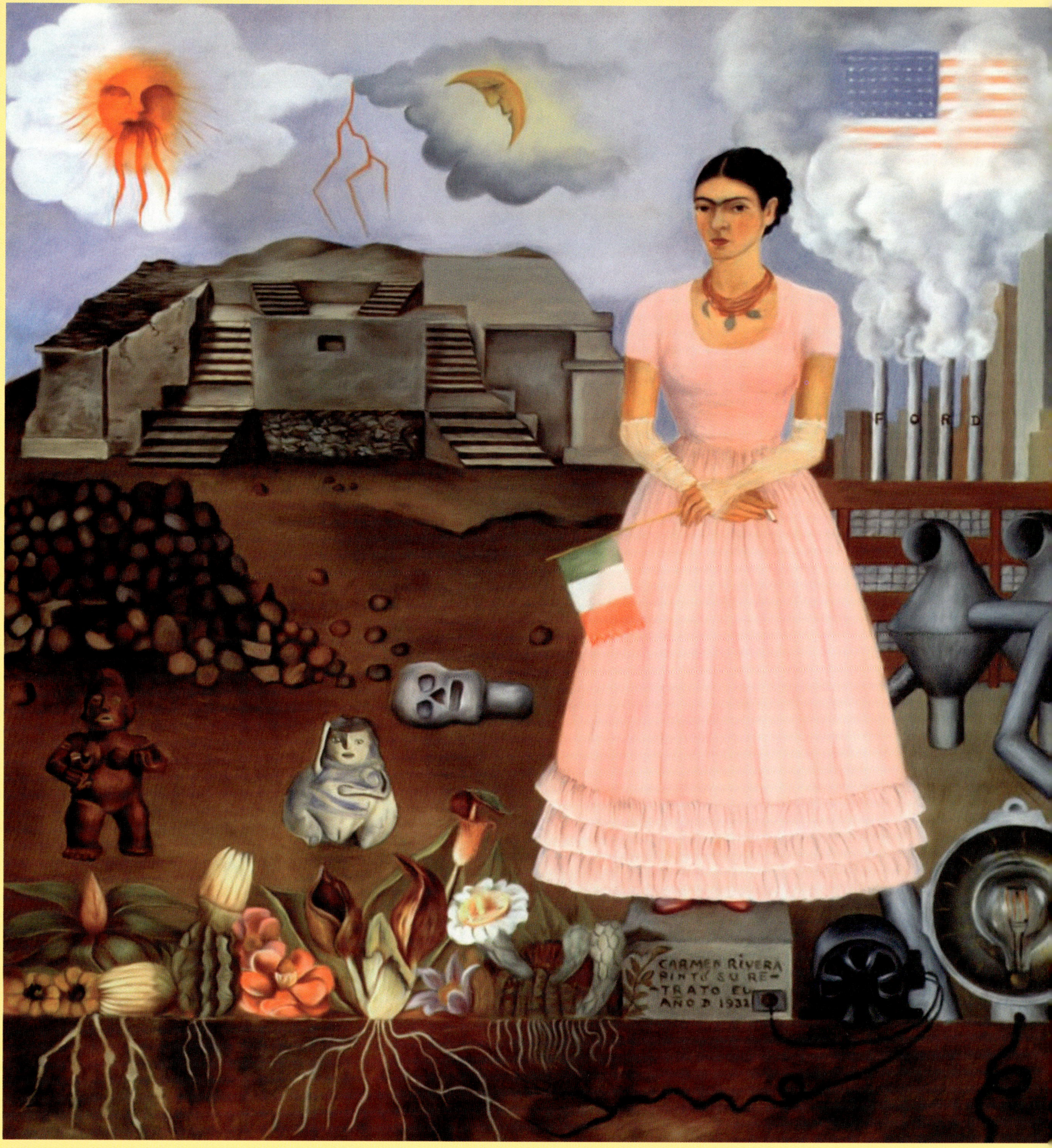
FORD
CARMEN RIVERA
PINTÓ SU RE-
TRATO EL
AÑO D 1932

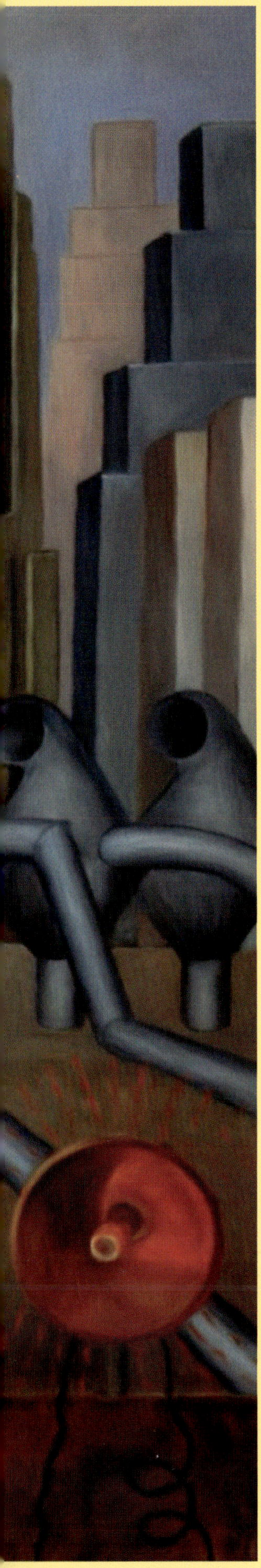

With Diego, Frida travelled the world. She moved to San Francisco in America with Diego for three years.

She worked hard to develop her folk art style. She loved meeting famous painters and authors. She travelled to New York and Detroit, where her art became recognised.

After three years, her health became delicate again.

'Diego, I don't feel well again. Let us go back to Mexico,' said Frida.

She had been trying to get pregnant but her body would not support her pregnancy.

Diego took Frida back to Mexico where she painted themes that interested her.

She soon became very famous. People all over the world recognised her.

One day, as she passed her old school, the hurtful comments of her classmates rang in her ears. Frida smiled and thought, *I told you I will be better than any of you.*

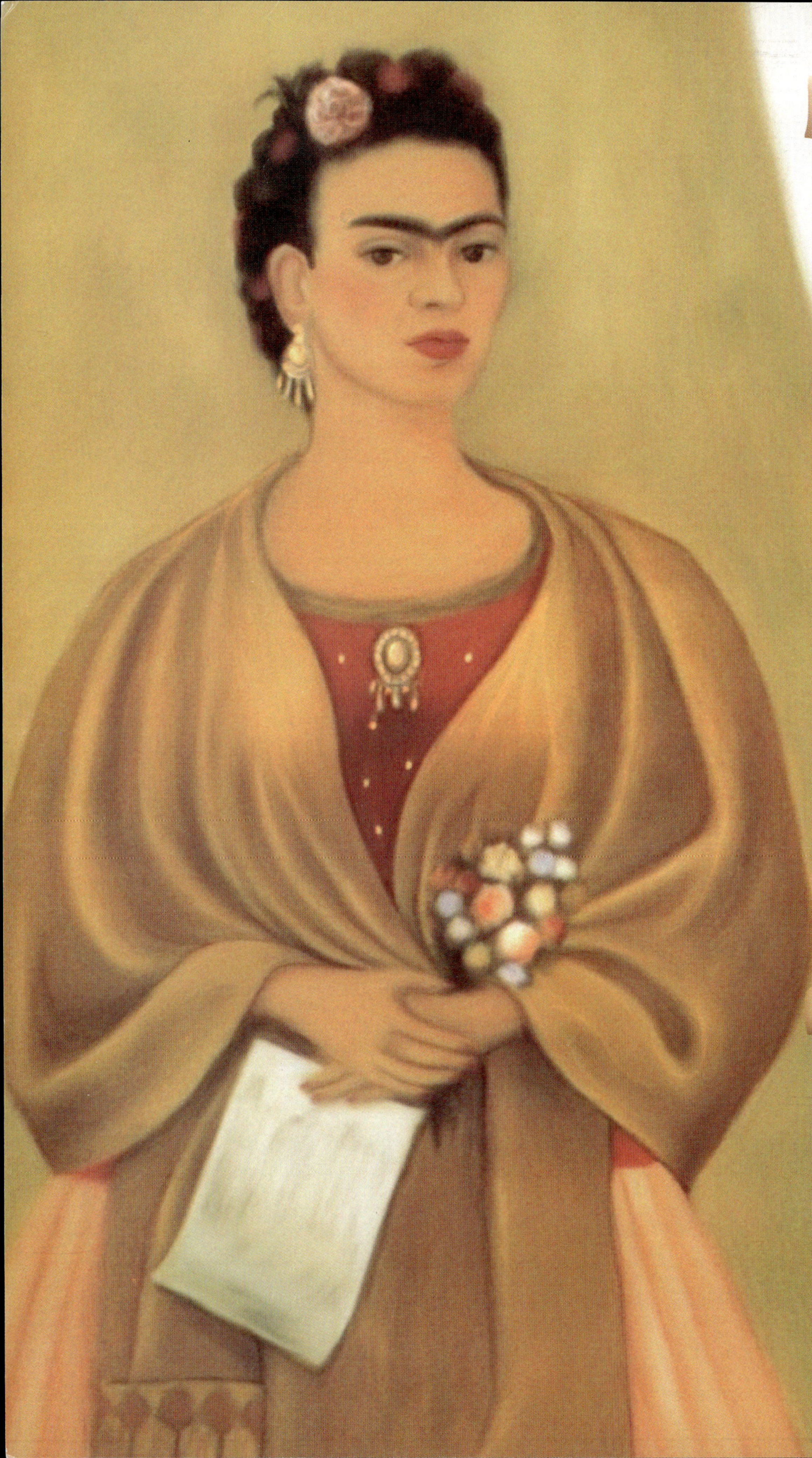

Frida was born in Coyocoan, Mexico City, Mexico on 6 July, 1907.

She studied in the National Preparatory School.

Frida and Diego Rivera were married in 1929.

In 1938, Frida had her first show in New York City, USA.

In 1939, she went to Paris to exhibit her work.

In 1939, she divorced Diego Rivera, only to remarry him in 1940.

Frida died on 13 July 1954, shortly after turning 47 in Mexico.

Frida's work remains one of the highest valued works by a female artist.